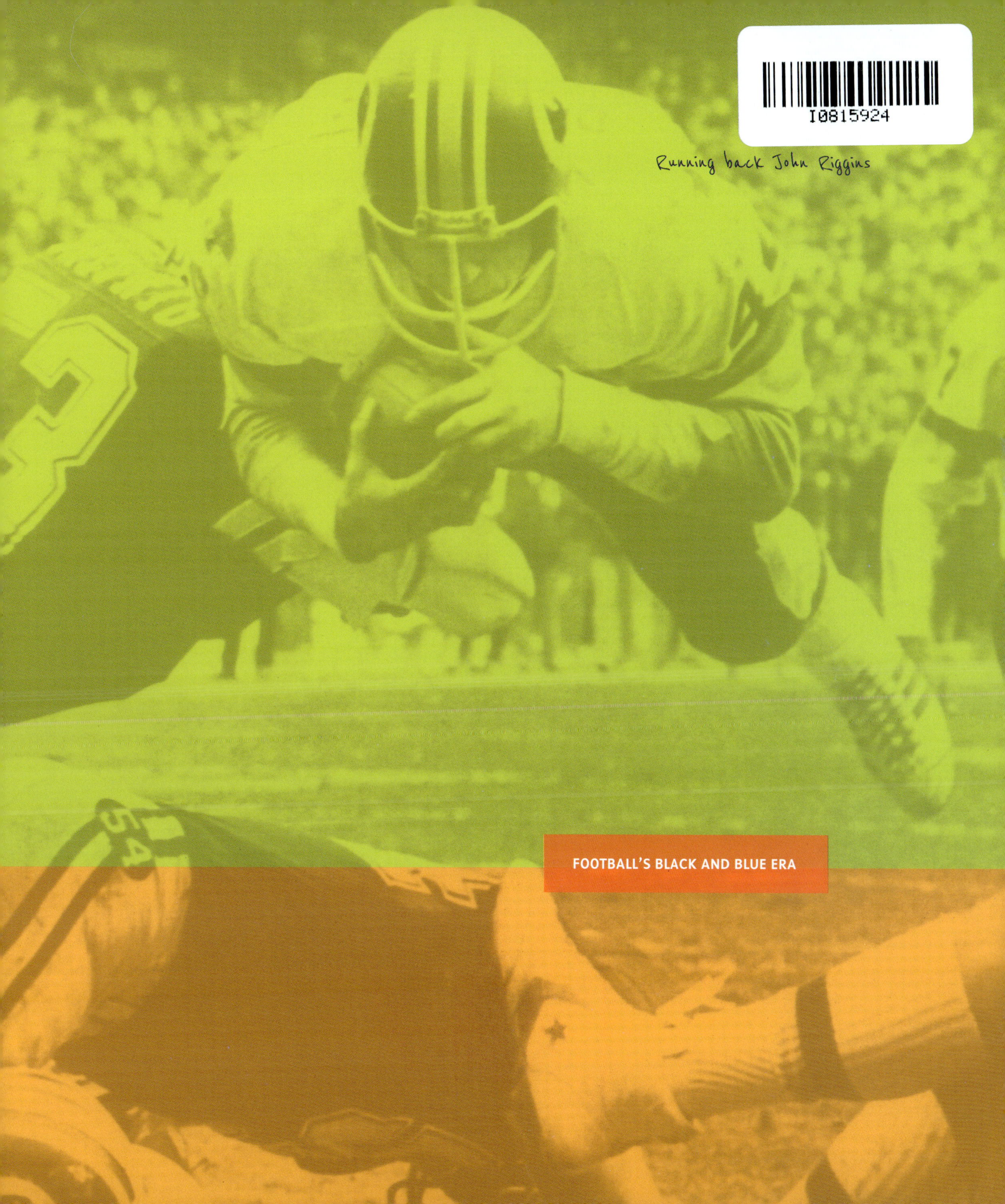
I0815924
Running back John Riggins
FOOTBALL'S BLACK AND BLUE ERA

Wide receiver Fred Biletnikoff, Super Bowl XI (11)

NFL SUPER BOWL STORIES

FOOTBALL'S BLACK AND BLUE ERA (1975–1984)

JAMES BARRY

Defensive tackle Joe Greene

CREATIVE EDUCATION / CREATIVE PAPERBACKS

Published by Creative Education and Creative Paperbacks
P.O. Box 227, Mankato, Minnesota 56002
Creative Education and Creative Paperbacks are imprints of The Creative Company
www.thecreativecompany.us

Design and production by Blue Design (www.bluedes.com)
Art direction by Graham Morgan
Edited by Kremena Spengler

Images by Associated Press/David Durochik, 29; Getty Images/ Al Messerschmidt Archive, 24, Andy Hayt, 7, B Bennett, 1, Bettmann, 16, 22, 26–27, Diamond Images, 15, Focus On Sport, cover, 3, 4–5, 6, 10, 12, 14, 19, 32, George Gojkovich, 25, George Rose, 7, John Iacono, 2, Jon Soohoo, 6, NFL/WireImage.com, 30, Otto Greule Jr, 7, Robert Riger, 7, Robin Alam/Icon Sportswire, 6, Ronald C. Modra, 20, Ross Lewis, 10, Wally McNamee, 9; NFL/ Manny Rubio/WireImage.com, 11, Vernon Biever, 6

Library of Congress Cataloging-in-Publication Data
Names: Barry, James (Author of children's books), author.
Title: Football's black and blue era (1975–1984) / James Barry.
Description: Mankato, Minnesota : Creative Education and Creative Paperbacks, [2026] | Series: Creative sports: NFL super bowl stories | Includes index. | Audience: Ages 8–12 | Audience: Grades 4–6 | Summary: "Terry Bradshaw, Bill Walsh, Jim Plunkett: Football's Black and Blue Era (1975–1984) was dominated by these names. Dramatic recaps introduce middle-grade readers to star NFL players from this era and ten exciting Super Bowls"– Provided by publisher.
Identifiers: LCCN 2024051455 (print) | LCCN 2024051456 (ebook) | ISBN 9798889896067 (library binding) | ISBN 9781682777725 (paperback) | ISBN 9798889896869 (ebook)
Subjects: LCSH: Football–United States–History–20th century–Juvenile literature. | Football players–United States–History–20th century–Juvenile literature. | National Football League–History–20th century–Juvenile literature.
Classification: LCC GV950.7 .B37 2026 (print) | LCC GV950.7 (ebook) | DDC 796.332/2–dc23/eng/20241122
LC record available at https://lccn.loc.gov/2024051455
LC ebook record available at https://lccn.loc.gov/2024051456

Printed in India

Defensive end Ed "Too Tall" Jones

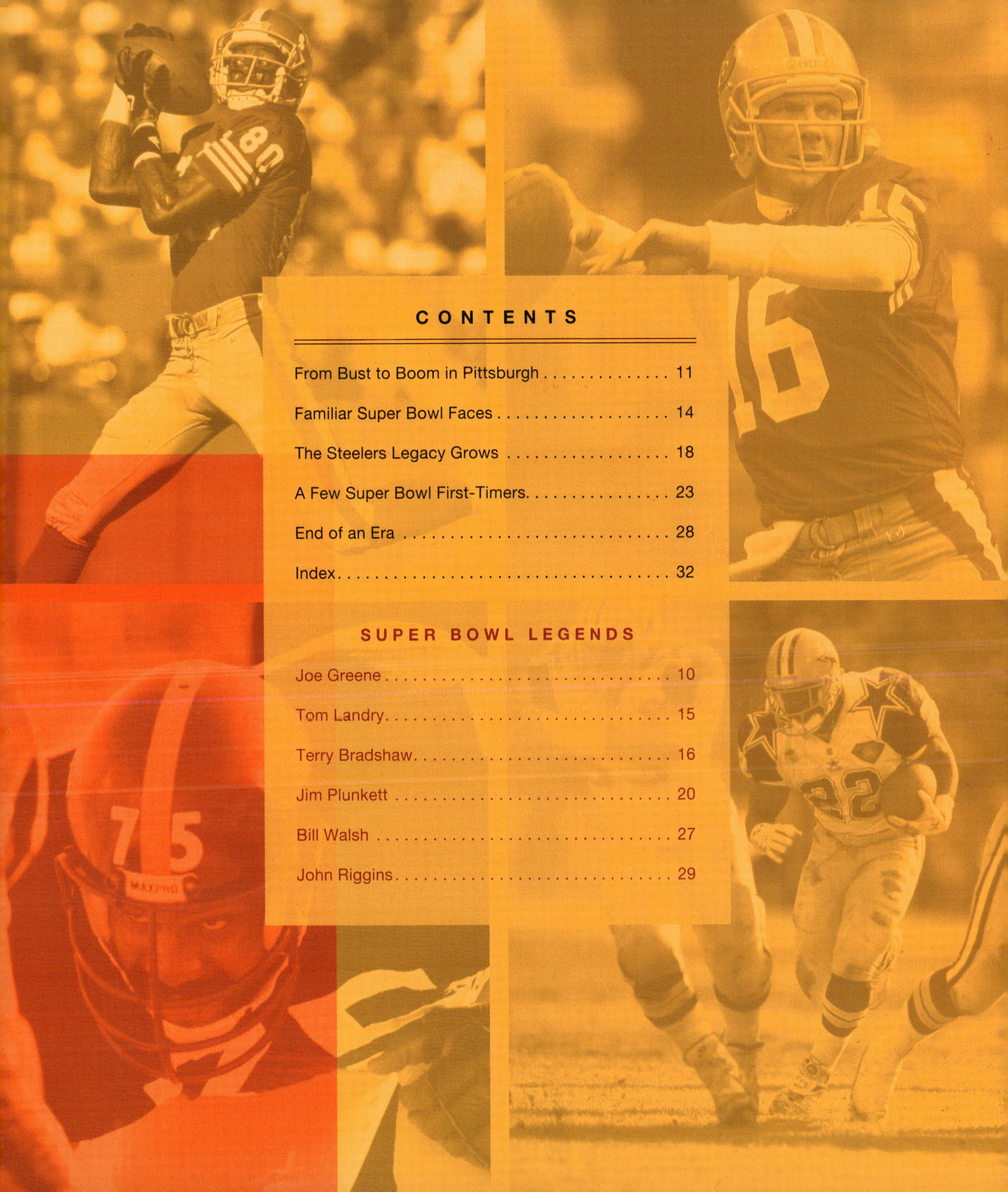

CONTENTS

SUPER BOWL LEGENDS

INTRODUCTION

It's the fourth quarter of Super Bowl XVII (17). The Miami Dolphins lead the Washington Redskins by a score of 17–13. But Washington has the ball in Miami territory. It's fourth down with one yard to go. Head coach Joe Gibbs decides to go for it. He knows exactly whom to trust: tough running back John Riggins. Riggins takes the handoff and breaks through the Miami defense. He doesn't just get the first down—he scores a 43-yard touchdown. The Redskins take the lead and never look back. They become Super Bowl champions.

Every team in the National Football League (NFL) wants to win the Super Bowl. It's the championship game between the best teams from each conference. In early Super Bowls, football was extra physical. Yards were hard to gain. Offenses didn't pass as much as they do now. The toughest teams usually won. Their heart-pounding plays tell the story of football's "Black and Blue Era."

Running back John Riggins, Superbowl XVII (17)

JOE GREENE

DEFENSIVE TACKLE
PITTSBURGH STEELERS, 1969–1981
6-FOOT-4, 275 POUNDS

"Mean" Joe Greene was one of the greatest defensive linemen in NFL history. Greene was known for his fierce style of play. That's how he earned his nickname. He won two NFL Defensive Player of the Year awards. He was head coach Chuck Noll's first draft pick in Pittsburgh. The Steelers won only one game in his first season. But he still won the Defensive Rookie of the Year award. Greene became the star of Pittsburgh's famous "Steel Curtain" defense. The Steelers often won low-scoring games with Greene and their defense taking charge. He won four Super Bowls with the Steelers.

Linebacker Jack Lambert

FROM BUST TO BOOM IN PITTSBURGH

The Pittsburgh Steelers faced the Minnesota Vikings in Super Bowl IX (9). The teams met at Tulane Stadium in New Orleans, Louisiana. It was a matchup of two great defenses on a slippery wet field.

The Vikings had suffered a big loss in Super Bowl VIII (8) to the Miami Dolphins. They were still seeking their first Super Bowl victory. They were led by head coach Bud Grant and veteran quarterback Fran Tarkenton. Their defensive linemen were called the "Purple People Eaters."

The Steelers were playing in their first Super Bowl. The team had struggled through years of losing seasons. But in 1969, owner Al Rooney had hired head coach Chuck Noll. He drafted great players like quarterback Terry Bradshaw and defensive tackle Joe Greene. In 1974, the Steelers became one of the best teams in the NFL. They finished with a 10–3–1 record. They were known for their "Steel Curtain" defense.

The game was a defensive battle. Vikings running back Dave Osborn fumbled a handoff from Tarkenton. The ball rolled backward into Minnesota's end zone.

Tarkenton recovered it to prevent a Steelers touchdown, but he was tackled for a safety. The Steelers led the Vikings 2–0 at halftime. It was the lowest halftime score in Super Bowl history.

The Steelers leaned on their running game in the second half. Fullback Franco Harris was the star of the offense. He scored the game's first touchdown early in the third quarter. Pittsburgh led 9–0 going into the fourth quarter. The Vikings came back into the game with a big play. They blocked a Steelers punt, and defensive back Terry Brown returned it for a touchdown. Kicker Fred Cox missed the extra point. The score was 9–6. But it wasn't enough. The Steelers came back with another touchdown drive. This one was led by Bradshaw. His touchdown pass to Larry Brown sealed the game.

The Steelers won Super Bowl IX (9) by a score of 16–6. Harris was named the Super Bowl's Most Valuable Player (MVP). He finished the game with 34 carries for 158 yards. Pittsburgh's defense dominated the game. The Vikings offense was held scoreless. Minnesota became the first team to lose three Super Bowls.

The Steelers returned in Super Bowl X (10) to face the Dallas Cowboys. It was a matchup of two great head coaches: Chuck Noll and Tom Landry. The two teams met at the Orange Bowl in Miami, Florida.

Dallas was the underdog in the game. Quarterback Roger Staubach was the leader of the team. Pittsburgh finished with the NFL's best record. Their "Steel Curtain" defense was stronger than ever. But the star of Super Bowl X (10) was Steelers wide receiver Lynn Swann.

Running back Franco Harris

Swann caught only four passes in the game. But they were four of the game's biggest plays. The biggest came in the fourth quarter. Quarterback Terry Bradshaw dropped back and threw a deep ball to Swann. He caught it for a 64-yard touchdown. It put the Steelers up 21–10 with under four minutes left. Swann finished with four catches for 161 yards and a touchdown. He was named Super Bowl X (10) MVP. The Steelers won back-to-back Super Bowls. One of the NFL's worst teams had turned itself into a dynasty.

Wide receiver Lynn Swann

FAMILIAR SUPER BOWL FACES

The Minnesota Vikings faced the Oakland Raiders in Super Bowl XI (11). It was the Vikings' fourth Super Bowl appearance. The Raiders were playing in their first. The two teams met at the Rose Bowl in Pasadena, California. There were more than 100,000 fans in attendance. The Vikings were still known for their "Purple People Eaters" defense. The Raiders won their last 10 games of the season to finish with the NFL's best record at 13–1. They were led by head coach John Madden.

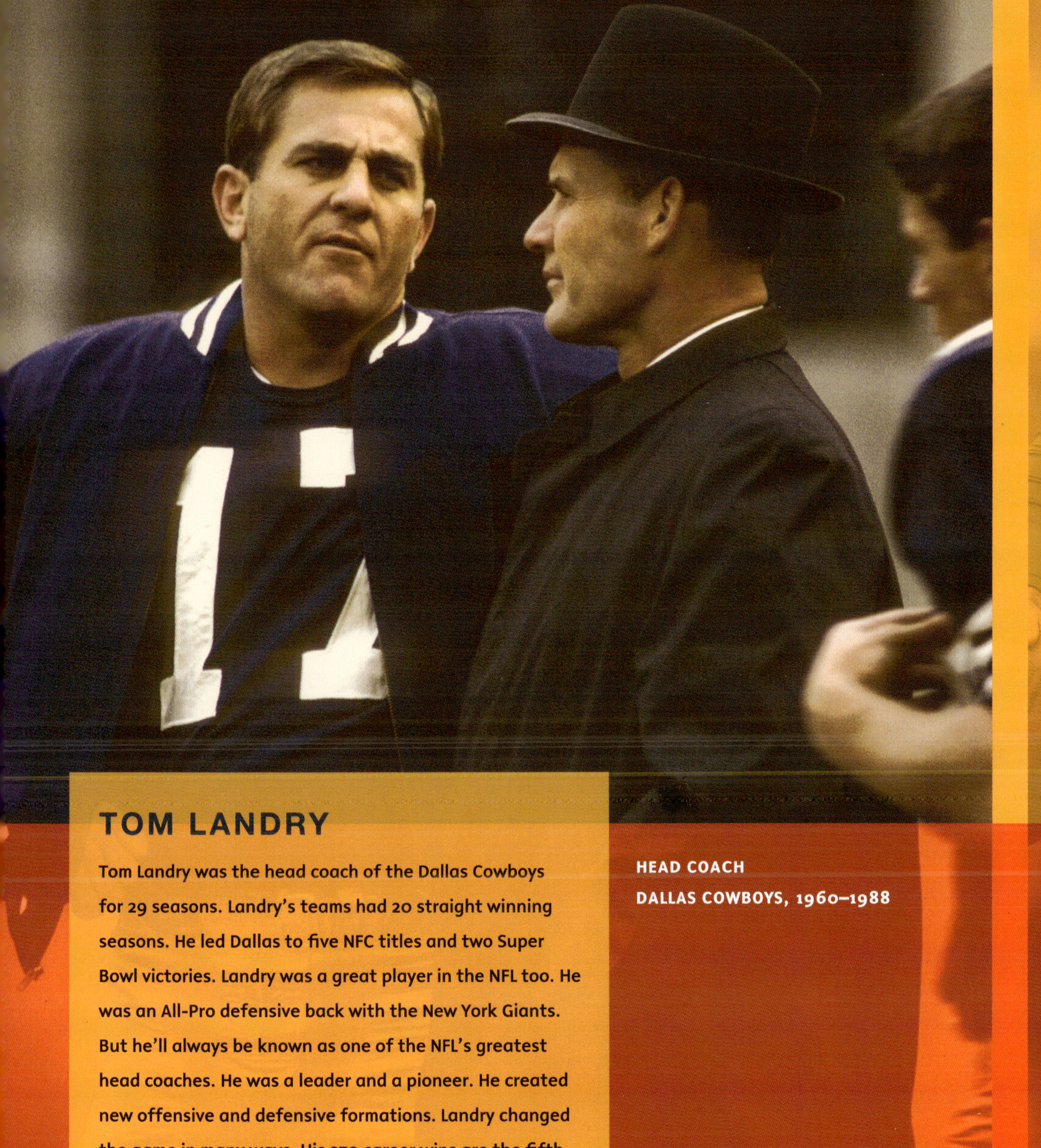

TOM LANDRY

Tom Landry was the head coach of the Dallas Cowboys for 29 seasons. Landry's teams had 20 straight winning seasons. He led Dallas to five NFC titles and two Super Bowl victories. Landry was a great player in the NFL too. He was an All-Pro defensive back with the New York Giants. But he'll always be known as one of the NFL's greatest head coaches. He was a leader and a pioneer. He created new offensive and defensive formations. Landry changed the game in many ways. His 270 career wins are the fifth most in NFL history.

HEAD COACH
DALLAS COWBOYS, 1960–1988

QUARTERBACK
PITTSBURGH STEELERS
1970–1983
6-FOOT-3, 215 POUNDS

TERRY BRADSHAW

Terry Bradshaw was the first overall pick in the 1970 NFL Draft. It took him a few years to adjust to the NFL. But with the guidance of head coach Chuck Noll, he figured things out. He led the Steelers to four Super Bowl victories. Bradshaw became the face of the Steelers dynasty. He had one of the strongest throwing arms ever. He loved to take risks and throw it deep. Many of the biggest plays in Pittsburgh's biggest wins were long balls from Bradshaw. The two-time Super Bowl MVP will always be known as a winner.

Oakland had one of the best offensive lines in the NFL. It was led by quarterback Ken Stabler. But in Super Bowl XI (11), it was the team's running game that shined. After a scoreless first quarter, the Raiders dominated the game. They took a 16–0 lead into halftime. Minnesota's offense was struggling. The Raiders were running all over the Vikings' defense. Oakland finished with 266 rushing yards. The offense finished with a Super Bowl record 429 total yards. The Raiders won Super Bowl XI (11) by a score of 32–14. The Vikings had lost another one. Coach Madden had turned the Raiders into winners.

Super Bowl XII (12) was between the Dallas Cowboys and the Denver Broncos. It was the Broncos' first Super Bowl. Tom Landry and the Cowboys were seeking their second Super Bowl victory. It was a matchup of two great defenses. The Cowboys' "Doomsday Defense" was the best in the National Football Conference (NFC). The Broncos' "Orange Crush" defense was the best in the American Football Conference (AFC). Both teams finished the season with a record of 12–2.

The game was also a matchup of two former teammates. Quarterbacks Roger Staubach and Craig Morton had spent years battling for the Cowboys starting job. Staubach finally won the job for good, and Morton went elsewhere. Would Morton get revenge? Or would Staubach prove Dallas made the right choice?

The Cowboys dominated Super Bowl XII (12). Their defense forced eight turnovers. They allowed only eight completions for 61 total passing yards. Morton threw as many interceptions as completions: four. Staubach threw for 183 yards and a touchdown. But it was the Cowboys' "Doomsday Defense" that won the game. Defensive tackle Randy White and defensive end Harvey Martin shared Super Bowl MVP honors. It was the first and only time two players shared the award. Dallas won its second Super Bowl.

THE STEELERS LEGACY GROWS

Super Bowl XIII (13) was the first Super Bowl rematch. Once again the Pittsburgh Steelers faced the Dallas Cowboys. Both teams had won two Super Bowls already. Both had legendary coaches, quarterbacks, and defenses. It was set to be one of the greatest NFL games of all time.

The game was called the "Battle of Champions." It took place at the Orange Bowl, where the Steelers had beaten the Cowboys in Super Bowl X (10). The Steelers started with a bang. Bradshaw completed a 28-yard touchdown pass to wide receiver John Stallworth. Staubach and the Cowboys answered late in the first quarter. Staubach threw a 39-yard touchdown of his own to wide receiver Tony Hill. The game was tied 7–7 after the first quarter. It never slowed down.

Early in the second quarter, Bradshaw lost a fumble. It was recovered and returned for a 37-yard touchdown. Three plays later, Bradshaw made up for it. He threw a 75-yard bomb to Stallworth for another touchdown. The game was tied again at 14–14. The entire game was action-packed. Bradshaw and Staubach combined for seven touchdowns and 546 passing yards.

It looked like it was over when Bradshaw completed his fourth touchdown pass of the game in the fourth quarter. The Steelers were up 35–17. But Staubach came back and threw two touchdown passes in the final three minutes. Unfortunately for the Cowboys, it wasn't enough. Pittsburgh won another Super Bowl. Bradshaw was named Super Bowl XIII (13) MVP. His 318 yards and four touchdowns were Super Bowl records.

Quarterback Terry Bradshaw

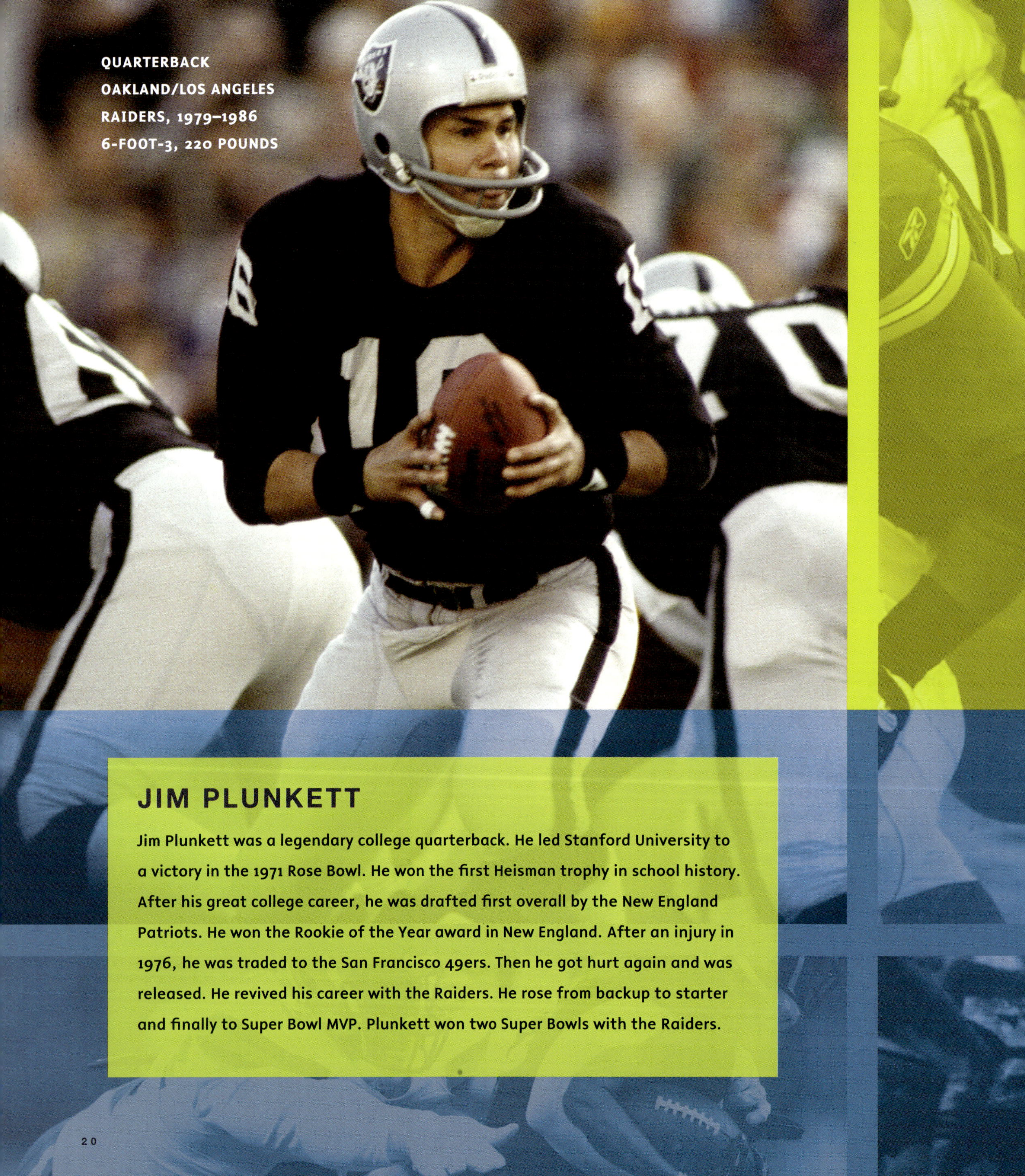

QUARTERBACK
OAKLAND/LOS ANGELES
RAIDERS, 1979–1986
6-FOOT-3, 220 POUNDS

JIM PLUNKETT

Jim Plunkett was a legendary college quarterback. He led Stanford University to a victory in the 1971 Rose Bowl. He won the first Heisman trophy in school history. After his great college career, he was drafted first overall by the New England Patriots. He won the Rookie of the Year award in New England. After an injury in 1976, he was traded to the San Francisco 49ers. Then he got hurt again and was released. He revived his career with the Raiders. He rose from backup to starter and finally to Super Bowl MVP. Plunkett won two Super Bowls with the Raiders.

The defending champion Steelers returned to Super Bowl XIV (14). This time they faced the Los Angeles Rams. Los Angeles was a big underdog in the game. It had finished the season with a 9–7 record. That was the worst ever by a team that reached the Super Bowl. The Rams had lost their starting quarterback Pat Haden to injury. He was replaced by Vince Ferragamo. Ferragamo threw twice as many interceptions as touchdowns in the regular season. But he led the Rams to the championship game.

The two teams met at the Rose Bowl. There were nearly 104,000 fans in attendance. That's still the largest crowd in Super Bowl history. The game was much closer than expected. The Rams led 13–10 after a back-and-forth first half. Things heated up in the third quarter. Bradshaw connected with wide receiver Lynn Swann for a 47-yard touchdown pass. The Steelers took the lead. The Rams answered right back. They scored a touchdown of their own on a special play. Running back Lawrence McCutcheon threw a 24-yard touchdown pass to wide receiver Ron Smith. Los Angeles led 19–17 after three quarters.

The play of the game came early in the fourth quarter. Bradshaw threw another deep ball. This time it was a 73-yard touchdown pass to John Stallworth. There were a record seven lead changes in the game. But once the Steelers retook the lead in the fourth quarter, they never gave it back. It was another Super Bowl MVP for Bradshaw. It was a record fourth Super Bowl victory for the Steelers. They became the NFL's top franchise.

83

A FEW SUPER BOWL FIRST-TIMERS

The Oakland Raiders faced the Philadelphia Eagles in Super Bowl XV (15). It was Oakland's third Super Bowl appearance and Philadelphia's first. The Eagles were expected to win despite the difference in team experience. They were led by head coach Dick Vermeil. Their defense led the league in fewest points allowed in the regular season. Oakland led in forced turnovers and interceptions.

The two teams met at the Louisiana Superdome in New Orleans, Louisiana. The first play of the game was an Eagles turnover. Eagles quarterback Ron Jaworski was intercepted by Raiders linebacker Rod Martin. Raiders quarterback Jim Plunkett threw a short touchdown pass to wide receiver Cliff Branch eight plays later. Before the end of the first quarter, Plunkett threw another touchdown pass. This one was an 80-yard completion to running back Kenny King. The Raiders led 14–0 after one quarter. They never looked back.

It was a rough game for Jaworski. He threw three interceptions and lost a fumble. All three interceptions were by Martin. That was a Super Bowl record. On the other side, it was a big game for Plunkett. He threw for 261 yards and three touchdowns. Plunkett was named Super Bowl XV (15) MVP. Once again the Raiders were Super Bowl champions.

Super Bowl XVI (16) saw two teams make it to the big game for the first time. It was the San Francisco 49ers against the Cincinnati Bengals. Both were surprise

Linebacker Rod Martin, Super Bowl XV (15)

Quarterback Ken Anderson

teams. The Bengals were led by quarterback Ken Anderson. He was the top-rated passer in the league. The 49ers were led by young quarterback Joe Montana. He finished the season with the league's highest completion percentage. It was set to be a close offensive battle.

The two teams met at the Pontiac Silverdome in Pontiac, Michigan. The 49ers started strong. Montana rushed for a touchdown and threw for one in the first half. San Francisco built a 20–0 lead heading into halftime. That was the biggest halftime lead in Super Bowl history. But in the second half, Anderson answered with a rushing touchdown and a passing touchdown of his own. After a San Francisco field goal, the Bengals trailed 23–14 in the fourth quarter. They had the ball with a chance to make it a one-score game. But on the first play of the drive, Anderson was intercepted by defensive back Eric Wright.

San Francisco kicked another field goal to build a 12-point lead with two minutes left. The Bengals scored again late, but the 49ers had put it away. Montana was named Super Bowl XVI (16) MVP. The 49ers had won their first Super Bowl. Head coach Bill Walsh was building something special in San Francisco.

Quarterback Joe Montana

16
56
68
87

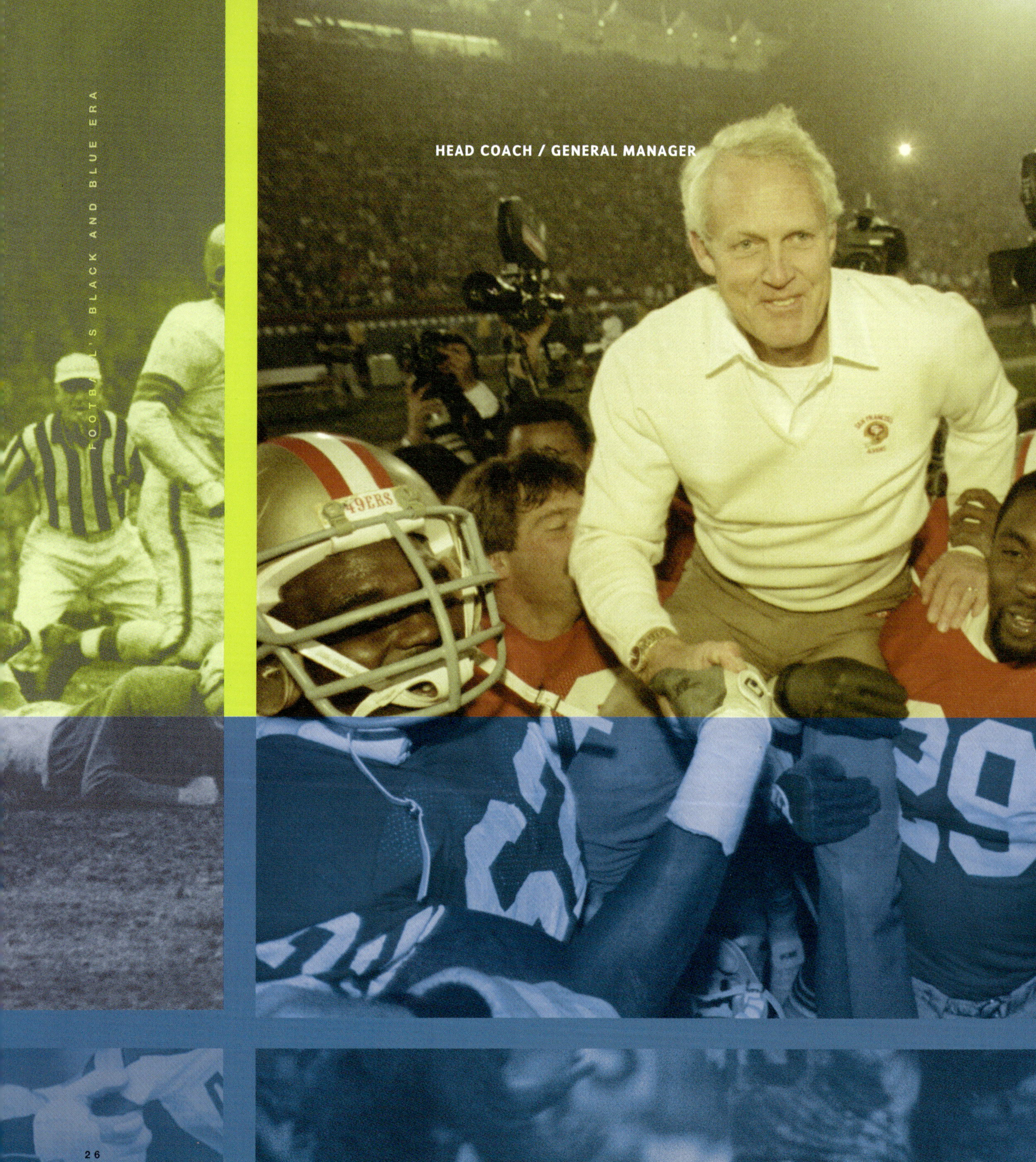
HEAD COACH / GENERAL MANAGER
49ERS

BILL WALSH

Bill Walsh was hired as the head coach and general manager of the 49ers in 1979. The team had just finished with a 2–14 record. They had won only 31 of their last 86 games. In three years, the 49ers were Super Bowl champions. Walsh posted a record of 102–63–1 in 10 seasons with San Francisco. He led the team to three Super Bowl victories. He was an offensive genius who helped many quarterbacks to great careers. Ken Anderson, Dan Fouts, and Joe Montana have all credited him for much of their success. He turned the 49ers into a dynasty.

END OF AN ERA

Super Bowl XVII (17) was the second ever Super Bowl rematch. The Miami Dolphins once again faced the Washington Redskins. The Dolphins entered with one of the NFL's best defenses. It was known as the "Killer Bees." The Redskins had a great offensive line. It was lovingly known as the "Hogs." It was expected to be a close game.

The teams met at the Rose Bowl. The Dolphins struck first. Quarterback David Woodley completed a 76-yard touchdown pass to wide receiver Jimmy Cefalo in the first quarter. The game was tight throughout the first half. The Redskins were leaning on running back John Riggins. The score was 10–10 with two minutes left in the half. Then the Dolphins hit Washington with another explosive play. Fulton Walker returned a Redskins kickoff 98 yards for a touchdown. Miami led 17–10 at halftime.

It was a one-score game in the fourth quarter. The Redskins trailed 17–13. It was fourth down with one yard to go in Miami territory. Head coach Joe Gibbs decided to go for it. The Redskins handed it to Riggins as they had all game. This time, he broke through the defense and took it all the way to the endzone for a 43-yard touchdown. It was the play of the game. Quarterback Joe Theismann threw a touchdown pass to seal the game with two minutes left. Riggins was named Super Bowl XVII (17) MVP. He set multiple Super Bowl records to finish one of the best postseasons of all time by a running back. The Redskins were NFL champions for the first time.

JOHN RIGGINS

John Riggins was one of the greatest postseason players of all time. He was a reliable running back known for his toughness. Riggins wasn't the fastest or the best. He was the steadiest. He always stepped up his game in the playoffs. He won a Super Bowl with the Redskins. He was named Super Bowl XVII (17) MVP. Riggins had one of the greatest postseasons ever that year. He rushed for 610 yards in four games. That's still the most rushing yards in a playoff season in NFL history. He helped give football's Black and Blue Era its name.

FULLBACK/RUNNING BACK
WASHINGTON REDSKINS, 1976–1985
6-FOOT-2, 230 POUNDS

Riddell
32

The Redskins defended their title in Super Bowl XVIII (18) against the Los Angeles Raiders. The Raiders had moved from Oakland in 1982. They were again led by head coach Tom Flores and quarterback Jim Plunkett. Only this time they had a new offensive weapon. His name was Marcus Allen, and he was the team's new running back. The Redskins entered the game as a dominant force. They had finished with the league's best record at 14–2. They allowed the fewest rushing yards in the league. They set the NFL record in scoring with 541 total points.

The two teams met at Tampa Stadium in Tampa, Florida. The first score of the game came from a blocked punt. LA's Derrick Jensen blocked a Washington punt and recovered it in the end zone for a touchdown. The Raiders never looked back.

LA forced three Washington turnovers. Meanwhile, Allen had a historic night running the ball. He scored two touchdowns and rushed for a Super Bowl record 191 yards—and against the NFL's best defense. He was named Super Bowl XVIII (18) MVP. The Raiders won by a score of 38–9. They scored the most points and won by the most points in Super Bowl history.

The Black and Blue Era was complete. Dynasties were built, and champions were crowned. A new era was on its way. The power of the passing game would soon be unleashed.

Running back Marcus Allen

INDEX